# French Toast Cookbook

*Delicious French Toast Recipes Made Easy*

# Table of Contents

# Introduction

First and foremost, I want to give you a massive *thank you* for purchasing my book, '*French Toast Cookbook: Delicious French Toast Recipes Made Easy.*'

You might be wondering why in the world I decided to write an entire book dedicated to French toast?

Or even how I even managed to fill these pages with unique and wondrous variations of this delicious food?

To be completely honest, it really wasn't all that difficult.

Well, let me rephrase that – it was a little bit difficult.

As in, finding the recipes and writing the book was certainly a whole lot of hard work.

However, it was also a whole lot of fun!

Did you know that the true origin of French toast remains almost completely unknown? Long before this sweet snack was even known as '*French toast*', similar recipes were being whipped up all around the world.

In fact, one of the earliest known variations of French toast has actually been traced all the way back to the Roman Empire, where bread soaked in a sweet egg mix was regularly served as an after dinner treat to weary soldiers.

What we do know for certain is that the name '*French toast*' was first coined in 17th-century England, where French immigrants developed a sound reputation for cooking this simple and delicious treat for dessert.

It was this traditional recipe (and obviously this name) that was first brought to America by the early settlers.

Interestingly, in France, this traditional dish is more commonly called *'pain perdu'* by the locals, which is loosely translated to *'lost bread'*. While the name 'lost bread' may sound a little odd, it makes sense if you take a second to think about it.

You see, when it first became a culinary staple in France, the local people made it from stale bread in order to save cost and limit food wastage.

Now, in modern day, French toast has truly evolved into a cuisine that sits apart from all others.

People use a variety of different breads to make French toast. In the western and southwestern United States, many cooks prefer sourdough bread. Within some Jewish-American communities in the New York area, people use leftover challah bread from the Sabbath dinner for French toast on Sunday mornings.

And this differs again when we start to look at it on a global scale.

In England and across the rest of the UK, French toast is often served savory, with the addition of ketchup a regular occurrence.

Alternatively, in New Zealand they prefer their French toast served with bananas, bacon and maple syrup (which is delicious, I might add). Similarly, Australians are renowned for their delicious sweet and savory variations of the famous dish.

While French toast was first eaten across Europe during the medieval times as a means to use up stale bread and reduce wastage, it has evolved into so much more.

To put it somewhat simply, there is now a whole world of French toast out there, just waiting to be explored – and I have complied them all in one place for your cooking pleasure.

In this cookbook, I have provided a vast number of amazing French toast recipes from across the globe. These recipes that will allow you to taste, experiment, and explore the wonderful world of French toast.

While some of these are traditional, and some of these are modern, I can assure you that they are all delicious.

So, what in the world are you waiting for? Let's get cooking!

# A

## Apple Pie French Toast

Servings: 8

### Ingredients:

- 9 medium-large eggs
- 4 medium apples (peeled and thinly sliced)
- 2 ½ tablespoons all-purpose flour
- 1 loaf thick-cut bread
- ½ teaspoon ground cinnamon
- ½ teaspoon vanilla extract
- ½ cup frozen butter
- ½ cup butter
- ½ cup brown sugar
- ½ cup white sugar
- ¼ cup water
- ¼ cup milk
- 1 teaspoon lemon juice, or as needed (optional)

### Method:

1. First, place apples in a bowl and drizzle with lemon juice to keep from browning.
2. Melt ½ cup butter in a large saucepan over medium heat; remove from heat. Stir flour into melted butter until smooth.
3. Return saucepan to low heat; stir in brown sugar, white sugar, and water until sugars dissolve and mixture is smooth, 3 to 5 minutes.

4. Increase heat to medium; cook and stir mixture until boiling. Reduce heat to low and add apples.
5. Simmer mixture until apples are cooked but slightly tender, 20 to 25 minutes.
6. Preheat griddle to 325 F (165 C).
7. Whisk eggs, milk, cinnamon, and vanilla extract together in a bowl. Dip bread slices into egg mixture until completely coated.
8. Grease heated griddle with frozen butter. Cook dipped bread slices on the hot buttered griddle until browned, 2 to 3 minutes per side.
9. Repeat with remaining frozen butter and dipped bread.
10. Serve French toast with apple mixture ladled over top.

*Note:*

- For varied textures, use more than one kind of apple. Depending on what variety of apple you use, time for cooking will differ.

# Avocado Stuffed French Toast

Servings: 4

## Ingredients:

- 8 slices challah bread or Hawaiian bread (sliced about 1½ inch thick)
- 4 eggs (poached or fried)
- 2 ripe avocados
- 2 medium-large eggs
- 2 tablespoons unsalted butter
- ½ teaspoon salt
- ½ cup milk
- ½ teaspoon hot sauce
- ¼ teaspoon pepper

## Method:

1. Mash avocado with salt and pepper in a small bowl.
2. Slice a horizontal slit in the bread along the longest side, all the way through to the back. Trying not to cut through around the bread. Stuff with ¼th of the mashed avocado per toast.
3. In a shallow, rectangular container, whisk together the eggs, milk, and hot sauce.
4. Melt butter on a griddle over medium-low heat. Dip the sandwiches in the egg mixture for a few seconds on each side. Cook the toast until golden brown, 2 to 3 minutes per side.
5. Top with a poached or fried egg.

# Almond-Crusted French Toast

Servings: 5

## Ingredients:

- 10 slices Italian bread (1 inch thick)
- 8 medium-large eggs
- 3 tablespoons sugar
- 1 teaspoon almond extract
- ½ cup 2% milk
- ½ teaspoon vanilla extract
- ½ cup almonds (sliced)
- confectioners' sugar and maple syrup

## Method:

1. Combine eggs, milk, sugar, almond and vanilla extract in a large bowl. Dip each slice of bread into egg mixture; place on waxed paper. Press almonds onto tops of bread slices.
2. Cook on a greased hot griddle for 3-4 minutes on each side or until golden brown.
3. Sprinkle with confectioners' sugar and serve with syrup.

# Angel Food Cake French Toast with Cream Cheese Maple Syrup

Servings: 8 slices

## Ingredients:

*For the French toast:*

- 1 package angel food cake (thawed)
- 4 medium-large eggs
- 1 teaspoon vanilla extract
- ½ teaspoon cinnamon
- 2/3 cup milk
- ¼ teaspoon salt

*For the syrup:*

- 3 ounces cream cheese
- 1 cup maple syrup
- ½ teaspoon cinnamon

## Method:

1. Start by slicing the angel food cake into 1 inch thick slices. Set aside.
2. In a shallow dish, such as a pie plate, whisk together the eggs, milk, vanilla, cinnamon, and salt until well combined.
3. Place as many slices of cake as will fit in the egg mixture and let sit 2 minutes per side.
4. While the cake is soaking, heat a skillet over medium-low heat. Spray with non-stick cooking spray.

5. Add a couple of slices of cake to the hot pan and cook for 4-5 minutes or until the bottom is golden brown.
6. Flip to the other side and repeat.
7. Repeat with the remaining slices of cake.
8. While the French toast is cooking, heat the maple syrup, cream cheese, and cinnamon in a small saucepan, whisking often. Whisk vigorously before pouring over the French toast.

## Bananas Foster French Toast

Yield: 8 servings

### Ingredients:

- 4 medium-large eggs
- 1 cup heavy cream
- 1 teaspoon cinnamon (ground)
- 8 tablespoons butter (divided)
- 8 large croissants (halved)
- ½ cup dark corn syrup
- ½ cup firmly packed brown sugar
- 1 cup maple syrup
- 1 cup pecans (chopped)
- 6 ripe bananas (halved crosswise and lengthwise)
- 1 teaspoon rum extract

### Method:

1. First, whisk together eggs, cream, and cinnamon in a shallow dish.
2. Melt 2 tablespoons butter in a large skillet over medium-high heat.
3. Dip 4 croissant halves in egg mixture to coat both sides. Using a fork, remove croissants from egg mixture, letting excess mixture drip off. Place croissant halves in hot skillet. Cook 2 to 3 minutes per side or until lightly browned.

4. Repeat procedure with remaining butter and croissant halves. Set aside and keep warm.
5. In a large skillet, combine corn syrup, brown sugar, maple syrup and pecans. Bring to a boil over medium-high heat. Reduce heat, and simmer for 2 minutes.
6. Add banana halves and rum extract. Coat with the syrup mixture, and simmer 1 minute. Spoon over French toast.
7. Serve immediately.

# BLT French Toast

Serves: 2-4

## Ingredients:

- 4 slices brioche bread (or 8 baguette slices)
- 4 roma tomato slices
- 4 lettuce leaves
- 4 medium-large eggs
- 2-3 tablespoons unsalted butter
- 2 tablespoons parmesan cheese
- 2 tablespoons flour
- 2 large slices applewood smoked bacon (cut in half)
- ¾ cup milk (or you can use cream or half and half)
- ¼ cup snipped fresh chives
- fresh ground salt and pepper

## Method:

1. The night before you plan to make it, set the sliced bread out on the counter to dry out slightly.
2. In the morning, preheat oven to 375. Place bacon on a rimmed baking sheet lined with foil. Cook until golden and crisp, about 15-20 minutes. Drain on paper towels. Reduce oven temperature to 200 degrees.
3. While bacon cooks, whisk together eggs, cream, chives, Parmesan, and flour. Season with salt and pepper.
4. Lay bread in a single layer in a large shallow dish and coat with egg mixture. Soak 20-30 minutes, turning once.

5. Melt butter in a large skillet over medium heat. When butter sizzles, add bread and cook until golden and crisp around edges, about 3-5 minutes per side, flipping once.
6. Transfer cooked pieces of bread to an oven safe plate in a warm oven until ready to serve.
7. To serve, layer tomato, lettuce, and bacon on a slice of French toast, and top with another slice or serve open-faced.

# Baked Egg (Toad in The Hole) French Toast

Yield: 8 pieces

## Ingredients:

- 8 slices of your favorite bread
- 8 large eggs
- 5 medium-large eggs (whisked)
- ½ teaspoon ground cinnamon
- ¼ cup milk (any kind)
- ¼ cup pure maple syrup
- ¼ teaspoon sea salt
- cooking spray
- sheet pan

## Method:

1. First, spray a sheet pan with cooking spray & set aside.
2. Pre-heat the oven to 350 F with the rack in the middle.
3. In a large bowl, mix together the 5 whisked eggs, milk, maple syrup, salt and cinnamon. Dip each piece of bread until it is fully coated. You can let them sit to soak a minute or so as well. Let excess egg drip off into the bowl.
4. Place bread on the sheet pan in a single layer. Cut out a shape in the middle of each piece of bread with a 1 ½ inch cookie cutter. You can place those cut out pieces around the pieces of dipped bread. Crack one egg carefully into the hole in each piece of bread.
5. Bake for 15-20 minutes depending on how runny you like your eggs.

# Banana Walnut French Toast

Serves: 9

## Ingredients:

- 18 slices French bread (half inch thick slices)
- 3 ripe bananas (cut into ¼ inch-thick slices)
- 3 medium-large eggs
- 3 tablespoons honey
- 2 tablespoons lemon juice
- 1 ¼ cups milk
- 1 tablespoon pure vanilla extract
- 1 cup walnuts (chopped)
- 1 teaspoon sugar
- ½ teaspoon cinnamon (ground)
- maple syrup

## Method:

1. Start by greasing a 3-quart rectangular baking dish; set aside.
2. In small bowl, gently toss bananas with lemon juice. Arrange half the bread slices in the bottom of the baking dish. Top bread with a layer of bananas. Add remaining bread slices.
3. Combine eggs, milk, honey, vanilla and cinnamon in a medium bowl. Slowly pour egg mixture over French bread to coat evenly. Press bread down lightly with the back of a spoon to moisten all the bread. Cover and refrigerate 8 to 24 hours.
4. Before baking, sprinkle with walnuts and sugar. Bake uncovered for 30 to 35 minutes at 325°F.

5. It is done when a knife inserted near center comes out clean. Top of bread should be light brown.
6. Serve with maple syrup.

# Blueberry Pie French Toast Muffins

Yield: 8

## Ingredients:

- 8 thick slices of whole grain bread (cut into cubes)
- 8 medium-large eggs
- 1 teaspoon vanilla extract
- ¾ cup milk
- ½ teaspoon lemon juice
- ¼ teaspoon lemon zest
- ¼ teaspoon ground allspice
- ¼ teaspoon salt
- ¼ cup blueberries

## Method:

1. First, preheat the oven to 350°F.
2. Grease 8 cups of a 12-cup muffin tin.
3. In a large bowl, whisk together the eggs, milk, vanilla, lemon zest, lemon juice, allspice and salt.
4. Add the bread cubes and stir, making sure all the cubes are covered in eggy mixture. Let soak for 5 minutes.
5. Fold in the blueberries. Spoon the bread mixture into muffin cups. Bake for 12 to 14 minutes, until the egg is cooked, and the muffins are golden brown. Turn out onto a rack to cool completely.
6. Store in an airtight container in the refrigerator for up to 1 week.

*Note:*

- This recipe lends itself to any seasonal fruit. To reheat, pop them into the toaster oven with the rack on the lowest level and heat them for 4 to 6 minutes. Serve with a drizzle of maple syrup or honey. If you're eating on the go, use a healthy smear of jam to avoid a sticky mess.

# Bacon Stuffed French Toast

Servings: 4

## Ingredients:

- 8 slices white bread (preferably stale)
- 8 slices bacon (cooked)
- 4 teaspoons butter
- 4 medium-large eggs
- 4 ounces cream cheese (softened)
- 1 teaspoon vanilla extract
- ½ cup milk
- 1/3 cup packed brown sugar
- vegetable oil

## Method:

1. Mix cream cheese and brown sugar in a medium bowl.
2. Spread one side of each slice of bread with cream cheese mixture.
3. Sandwich 2 slices of bacon between 2 pieces of bread with the cream cheese side facing in. Repeat for remaining slices of bread to make a total of four.
4. In a shallow bowl, whisk together eggs, milk, and vanilla extract.
5. Dip each French toast "sandwich" in egg mixture. Try to only get the egg mixture on the exterior of each piece of bread and not let it soak through to the middle where the bacon is or it will turn out soggy, plus any egg that gets in the middle won't really cook.

6. Heat a large nonstick pan or griddle over medium heat. Add butter and a little vegetable oil. Cook each stuffed French toast until golden brown on bottom and then flip over. Add more butter and oil to pan if necessary. Cook until second side is golden brown.
7. Cut each piece in half and serve with maple syrup.

# Baked French Toast Sticks

Servings: 4

## Ingredients:

- 8 slices thick cut Texas toast bread
- 3 medium-large eggs
- 2 tablespoons sugar
- 2 teaspoons vanilla extract
- 1 ½ cups whole milk
- 1 teaspoon ground cinnamon
- cooking spray
- maple syrup (for serving)

## Method:

1. First, preheat the oven to 350°F.
2. Line a baking sheet with foil and grease it with cooking spray.
3. Cut each slice of bread into three sticks widthwise.
4. In a large shallow dish or bowl, whisk together the eggs, milk, cinnamon, sugar and vanilla extract. Dip each stick of bread in the egg mixture, coating it on all sides, then shake off the excess and arrange it on the baking sheet.
5. Repeat the dipping process, arranging the French toast sticks on the baking sheet so that they aren't touching.
6. Bake the French toast sticks for 12 minutes then flip them once, spray them lightly with cooking spray and return them to the oven for an additional 12 to 15 minutes or until cooked through.

7. Remove the French toast sticks from the oven and serve warm with maple syrup.

# C

## Creme Brulee French Toast with Drunken Strawberries

Serves: 4-6

### Ingredients:

- 1-quart strawberries (hulled and sliced ¼-inch thick, lengthwise)
- 5 medium-large eggs
- 2 teaspoons grand marnier or cointreau
- 2 tablespoons corn syrup
- 1 cup brown sugar (packed)
- 1 loaf challah or brioche bread (sliced into 1 ½-inch thick slices)
- 1 teaspoon vanilla
- ¾ cup heavy cream
- ¾ cup milk
- ½ cup butter, unsalted (1 stick)
- ¼ teaspoon salt
- ¼ cup sugar
- ¼ cup grand marnier or Cointreau
- powdered sugar (optional)

### Method:

1. First, butter a 9 by 13 baking dish.
2. Melt the butter with the brown sugar and corn syrup in a small pot. Stir together until the sugar is completely melted. Pour mixture into the baking dish.

3. Place the bread slices on top of the butter and sugar mixture in one even layer. Squeeze the edges slightly to make the bread fit.
4. In a bowl, whisk together the eggs, cream, milk, vanilla, salt, and 2 teaspoons of Grand Marnier. Pour this mixture over the bread. Tightly cover baking dish with plastic wrap and refrigerate for 8 hours or overnight.
5. Let dish stand at room temperature for 20 minutes before placing in the preheated oven at 350 F.
6. Bake for 30 to 40 minutes until French toast is golden and puffed.
7. Serve hot with drunken strawberries and powdered sugar sprinkled on top.

*Make the Drunken Strawberries:*

1. Combine sliced strawberries, sugar, and Grand Marnier in a small bowl.
2. Cover with plastic wrap and refrigerate for 2 hours up to 24 hours.

# Classic French Toast

Servings: 8

## Ingredients:

- 8 thick slices bread
- 4 medium-large eggs
- 1 teaspoon ground cinnamon
- 1 teaspoon vanilla extract
- 2/3 cup milk
- ¼ cup all-purpose flour
- ¼ cup granulated sugar
- ¼ teaspoon salt

## Method:

1. First, preheat griddle to 350 F or heat a skillet over medium heat. Grease well with butter.
2. Add all ingredients, except the bread, to a blender or to a shallow dish and whisk well to combine. If whisking by hand, it's okay if the flour doesn't mix in completely smooth.
3. Dip bread slices into the egg mixture, dredging them well on both sides, and place on hot, greased griddle or skillet.
4. Cook for a few minutes, until the bottom of the breads starts to get golden brown. Flip and cook on the other side the same.
5. Remove to a plate. Serve warm, with syrup and a sprinkle of powdered sugar.

# Cinnamon Sugar French Toast

Serves: 4

## Ingredients:

- 2 medium eggs
- 1 ½ teaspoons cinnamon (divided)
- 1 loaf sourdough bread
- 1 cup milk
- ½ teaspoon sugar
- ¼ cup confectioners' sugar
- 1/8 teaspoon salt
- butter or oil
- maple syrup
- butter

## Method:

1. First, combine milk, sugar, eggs, ½ teaspoon cinnamon, and salt and mix until blended.
2. Cut bread into ¾ inch slices.
3. Dip in milk/egg mixture long enough to soak through.
4. Place a hot skillet with the melted butter or oil and fry until golden brown on both sides.
5. Remove from pan and roll in confectioners' sugar mixed with the remaining cinnamon.
6. Serve with syrup and butter.

# Cinnamon Vanilla Baked French Toast

Servings: 6-10

## Ingredients:

*French toast:*

- one 15 oz loaf French bread cut into large cubes (preferably a day or two old)
- 8 medium-large eggs
- 1 ½ teaspoons ground cinnamon
- 1 tablespoon pure vanilla extract
- 1 cup whole milk
- 1 cup half and half
- ½ cup brown sugar

*Topping:*

- 6 tablespoons unsalted butter (softened)
- 1 teaspoon ground cinnamon
- ¼ teaspoon salt
- 2/3 cup brown sugar
- 2/3 cup all-purpose flour
- maple syrup (for serving)

## Method:

*Preparation (allow time to soak overnight):*

1. First, place the bread cubes in a greased casserole dish (I used a 2 ½-quart dish).
2. Whisk eggs, milk, half and half, brown sugar, cinnamon, and vanilla in a large bowl. Pour evenly over the bread cubes.

3. Lightly press down on the top of the bread to allow the top layer of bread to absorb some of the custard mixture, or gently stir it to distribute the custard throughout the bread.
4. Cover, and refrigerate overnight (if you want to bake the same day, allow it to soak for at least 3 hours).

*For the topping:*

1. Combine brown sugar, flour, cinnamon and salt. Add butter, and using your fingers or a spoon, work the butter into the dry ingredients until the butter is evenly distributed and the mixture resembles wet, clumpy sand. Cover and refrigerate until you are ready to bake the French toast.

*Baking:*

1. Preheat oven to 350°F.
2. Remove the French toast from the refrigerator (the bread will have absorbed most of the custard).
3. Crumble the topping over the top of the French toast. Bake uncovered for 40-55 minutes, until puffed, golden brown, and set (check that the center is not too wet).
4. Baking time will depend on how deep your casserole dish is and whether you prefer your french toast more well done.
5. Serve immediately with maple syrup. Leftovers can be refrigerated.

# Caramelized Apple French Toast

Serves: 4

## Ingredients:

- 8 1/2-inch-thick slices white bread
- 2 medium-large eggs
- 2 tablespoons dark rum
- 1 cup low-fat (1%) milk
- 1 teaspoon unsalted butter
- 1 teaspoon pure vanilla extract
- 1 teaspoon ground cardamom
- ¼ cup dark brown sugar
- ¼ cup + 2 tablespoons unsweetened applesauce
- ¼ cup granulated sugar
- pinch of salt

## Method:

1. Preheat the oven to 375°.
2. Lightly grease a large nonstick baking sheet with the butter.
3. Press the brown sugar through a strainer onto a medium plate to remove any lumps and then sprinkle 2 tablespoons of the sugar evenly over the prepared baking sheet.
4. Whisk the milk with the eggs, applesauce, granulated sugar, rum, vanilla, cardamom, and salt in a shallow bowl.
5. Add the bread slices and turn to coat, until thoroughly moistened. Arrange the slices on the

prepared baking sheet and sprinkle evenly with the remaining 2 tablespoons brown sugar.

6. Bake for about 20 minutes, turning once, until the toast is lightly browned, and the sugar is caramelized.

7. Transfer the French toast to plates and serve.

# Custard French Toast

Yield: 8-10 servings

## Ingredients:

- 8-10 slices day-old French bread (1 inch thick)
- 5 tablespoons butter (melted)
- 4 medium-large eggs
- 3 cups milk
- 2 egg yolks
- 1 cup heavy whipping cream
- 1 tablespoon vanilla extract
- ½ cup sugar
- ¼ teaspoon ground nutmeg
- confectioners' sugar (optional)

## Method:

1. Start by brushing both sides of bread with butter; place in a greased 13x9-in. baking dish.
2. Beat eggs and yolks in a large bowl. Add milk, cream, sugar, vanilla and nutmeg; mix well. Pour over the bread slices. Cover and chill overnight.
3. Remove from the refrigerator 30 minutes before baking.
4. Bake, uncovered, at 350° for 55-60 minutes or until a knife inserted in the center comes out clean.
5. Cool 10 minutes before serving. Dust with confectioners' sugar if desired.

# Cornflake Crusted French Toast

Servings: 12

## Ingredients:

- 12 slices Texas toast (sliced diagonally into triangles)
- 8 cups cornflakes (crushed)
- 2 ½ teaspoons baking powder
- 2 cups milk
- 2 medium eggs
- 1 cup all-purpose flour
- ½ teaspoon cinnamon
- ½ teaspoon salt
- ½ teaspoon vanilla extract
- ¼ cup sugar
- vegetable oil (for frying)
- syrup, whipped cream, and fruit (for serving)

## Method:

1. First, preheat oven to 200 F.
2. whisk together milk, eggs, sugar, cinnamon, salt, and vanilla in a large shallow bowl until well blended. Slowly whisk in flour and baking powder until smooth.
3. Add cornflakes to a second shallow bowl and place next to the batter. Heat 1-inch oil in a heavy skillet to 325 degrees.
4. Working with 1 or 2 bread slices at a time, dip bread in batter and allow any excess to drip off and back into the bowl.

5. Roll generously in cornflake crumbs. Immediately fry in oil until golden brown, about 1 minute per side.
6. Drain on paper towels and transfer to a baking sheet in oven to keep warm. Repeat with remaining bread slices.
7. Serve warm with your favorite toppings such as maple syrup, powdered sugar, whipped cream, fresh fruit, or candied pecans.

# Churro French Toast

Servings: 6

## Ingredients:

- 5 medium-large egg yolks
- 2 ¼ cups 2% milk
- 1 package (3 ounces) cook-and-serve vanilla pudding mix
- 1-3/4 teaspoons ground cinnamon, divided
- 1/4 teaspoon salt
- 1/2 cup sugar
- 12 slices French bread (1-1/4-inch thick)
- 1 can (13.4 ounces) dulce de leche, warmed, optional
- 2 tablespoons water, optional

## Method:

1. First, whisk egg yolks, milk, pudding mix, ½ teaspoon cinnamon and salt in a shallow bowl until blended.
2. In another shallow bowl, whisk sugar and remaining cinnamon.
3. Lightly grease a griddle; heat over medium heat. Dip both sides of bread in egg mixture. Place on griddle; toast 3-4 minutes on each side or until golden brown.
4. Dip in cinnamon sugar. If desired, mix dulce de leche and water; drizzle over toast.

# Coconut Banana Vegan French Toast

Servings: 4-6

## Ingredients:

- 4 - 6 slices day old bread
- 1 large banana
- 1 tablespoon maple syrup (plus more for serving)
- 1 teaspoon vanilla extract
- 1 tablespoon vegan butter or light oil for frying
- ¾ cup full-fat coconut milk
- ½ teaspoon cinnamon

## Method:

1. In a food processor or blender, add the banana, coconut milk, maple syrup, vanilla extract, and cinnamon. Blend to a smoothie-like consistency.
2. Pour your French toast dip into a shallow bowl that will fit your slices of bread.
3. Heat the vegan butter in a non-stick frying pan over medium heat. When hot, dip a slice of bread into the batter and coat both sides.
4. Place the bread in a hot pan and fry for a couple of minutes per side until golden brown.

# Crunchy French Toast

Servings: 4

## Ingredients:

- 4 thick slices bread
- 3 medium-large eggs
- 3 tablespoons granulated sugar
- 2 heaping cups corn flakes cereal
- 2 tablespoons all-purpose flour
- 1-2 tablespoons butter
- ½ teaspoon ground cinnamon
- ½ teaspoon vanilla extract
- 1/3 cup milk
- ¼ teaspoon salt

## Method:

1. First, add the eggs, milk, flour, sugar, salt, cinnamon, and vanilla in a shallow pie dish and whisk well to combine.
2. Place the corn flakes in a zip-lock bag and crush with your hands or a rolling pin until they are about the size of rolled oats. Spread the crushed corn flakes into another shallow dish.
3. Dip each piece of bread into the egg mixture and then press gently into the crushed corn flakes, flipping to coat both sides.
4. Melt a small piece of butter in a skillet over medium heat; add the bread and cook for 2-3 minutes on one side, until golden, and then flip and cook on the other side.
5. Serve with your favorite syrup and fruit.

# Croissant French Toast

Servings: 8

## Ingredients:

*Blackberry syrup:*

- 1-pint fresh blackberries
- 2 tablespoons cornstarch
- 1 cup sugar

*Croissant French toast:*

- 8 croissants (a rounder shape is best)
- 5 medium-large eggs
- 2 tablespoons sugar
- 2 teaspoons vanilla extract
- 1 teaspoon ground cinnamon
- ¼ cup half-and-half
- butter (for frying and serving)
- warm maple syrup (for serving)
- strawberries (for serving)
- whipped cream (for serving)

## Method:

*For the blackberry syrup:*

1. Combine the blackberries, sugar and ½ cup water in a saucepan. Bring to a gentle boil and cook for 5 minutes on low.
2. Stir in the cornstarch, then continue cooking, using a whisk or spoon to mash the larger pieces of blackberries. Remove from the heat when it's nice and thick.

*For the croissant French toast:*

1. Split the croissants in half through the middle.
2. In a bowl, whisk together the half-and-half, sugar, vanilla, cinnamon and eggs.
3. Dunk each croissant half into the mixture so that it's fully coated. Set the pieces aside on a plate.
4. Heat a large nonstick skillet over low heat, then melt a small amount of butter in it. Add as many croissant halves as will fit, cut-side down, then increase the heat very slightly (don't go above medium low).
5. Allow the pieces to cook on the first side for 3 to 4 minutes. Move them around in the skillet a bit to make sure they don't burn. When they're deep golden brown on the bottom, flip them to the other side and let them cook for another 2 minutes or so. Remove from the pan and cook the rest of the croissant halves.
6. Serve a top and bottom piece together with butter, warm blackberry syrup and maple syrup, strawberries and whipped cream.

# Cheesecake French Toast

Servings: 4

## Ingredients:

- 4 ounces cream cheese (softened)
- 4 hamburger buns
- 1 ½ cups cinnamon graham crackers (crushed)
- 1 teaspoon + a splash of vanilla (divided)
- 1 large egg
- ½ cup milk
- ¼ cup sugar

## Method:

1. First, mix cream cheese, sugar, and 1 teaspoon vanilla in a small bowl until smooth.
2. Make sandwiches with the cream cheese mixture using the hamburger buns.
3. Add milk, splash of vanilla, and egg to a shallow dish or bowl. Whisk well. Place graham cracker crumbs in a second shallow dish.
4. Heat griddle or frying pan over medium-low heat. Spray with cooking spray or melt butter on the hot surface to prevent sticking.
5. Dip each sandwich in the egg, turning to coat completely. Then dip the sandwich in the graham cracker crumbs and turn to coat, being sure to get the sides, top, and bottom covered with the crumbs.
6. Place each sandwich on the griddle and press it down with a spatula to flatten slightly.
7. Cook about 1-2 minutes on each side, until golden.
8. Serve hot with syrup, if desired.

# Cannoli Stuffed French Toast

Servings: 2

## Ingredients:

- 4 slices French bread
- 2 medium-large eggs
- 2 tablespoons butter
- 1 cup ricotta cheese
- ½ teaspoon vanilla extract
- 1/3 cup semi-sweet chocolate chips
- ¼ cup powdered sugar
- ¼ cup heavy cream (or milk)
- powdered sugar (for serving)

## Method:

1. First, combine the ricotta cheese, powdered sugar, and vanilla extract in a small bowl. Stir in the mini chocolate chips. Set aside.
2. In a shallow bowl or pie plate, whisk the eggs and heavy cream together.
3. Spread 2 slices of the bread with the ricotta mixture, about ½ cup per slice. Place the other slices of bread on top and gently press them together.
4. Carefully dip both sides of each sandwich into the egg mixture until well coated.
5. In a large skillet, melt the butter. Add the French toast sandwiches and cook until golden, about 4 minutes per side.
6. Cut the sandwiches in half on the diagonal and transfer to plates.
7. Dust with confectioners' sugar and serve immediately.

# D

## Deep Dish French Toast

Yield: 6-8

### Ingredients:

- 1 (24-ounce) brioche loaf (cut into 1-inch cubes)
- 1 (8-ounce package cream cheese (cut into 18 cubes)
- 8 medium-large eggs
- 4 tablespoons butter (melted)
- 2 teaspoons vanilla
- 2 cups milk
- 1 teaspoon cinnamon
- ¾ cup pecans or walnuts (chopped)
- ½ cup raisins
- ½ cup firmly packed dark brown sugar
- pinch of nutmeg
- pinch of cloves

### Method:

1. First, generously butter a 9-x-13-inch baking dish.
2. Place half the bread cubes in a single layer, filling in all the gaps. Evenly scatter the cream cheese cubes, nuts, and raisins on top. Cover completely with the remaining bread cubes.
3. In a large bowl, whisk together the eggs, milk, brown sugar, vanilla, cinnamon, nutmeg, and cloves. Evenly pour the egg mixture over the bread cubes. Gently press down on the cubes with your

palms to allow the top layer of bread to absorb the liquid. Cover with plastic wrap and refrigerate four hours or overnight.

4. Heat the oven to 350°F (175°C).

5. In the meantime, remove the dish from the refrigerator and let sit 20 minutes at room temperature. Bake the French toast covered for 20 minutes; uncover and bake 15 to 20 minutes longer, or until the cubes are nicely toasted and there's no liquid puddling on the bottom.

6. Transfer the dish to a rack and drizzle the melted butter on top. Run a knife around the rim of the pan to release the French toast. Let sit 5 minutes.

7. Cut into squares, arrange on individual plates, sprinkle with powdered sugar, and serve along with the warmed maple syrup.

# Doughnut French Toast

Yield: 2 servings

## Ingredient
s:

- 4 teaspoons vanilla extract
- 4 slices from a small white loaf or 2 slices from a large white loaf, each large slice cut in half
- 2 large eggs
- 1-ounce butter (plus a drop flavorless oil, for frying)
- ½ cup full fat milk
- ¼ cup sugar

## Method:

1. First, beat the eggs with the milk and vanilla in a wide shallow bowl.
2. Soak the bread halves in the eggy mixture for 5 minutes a side.
3. Heat the butter and oil in a frying pan/skillet, fry the egg-soaked bread until golden and scorched in parts on both sides.
4. Put the sugar onto a plate and then dredge the cooked bread until coated like a sugared doughnut.

# E

## Eggnog French Toast

Serves: 4

### Ingredients:

- 8 slices challah or bread of your choice
- 2 tablespoons (30 ml) unsalted butter
- 2 medium-large eggs
- 1 teaspoon (5 ml) vanilla
- ½ cup (125 ml) eggnog (store bought or homemade)
- ¼ teaspoon (1.25 ml) ground cinnamon
- ¼ teaspoon (1.25 ml) freshly ground nutmeg
- pinch salt
- maple syrup
- fresh assorted berries

### Method:

1. Whisk eggs, eggnog, cinnamon, nutmeg, salt and vanilla in a bowl.
2. Dip challah slices in egg mixture, soaking for 10 seconds. Let excess drip off.
3. Melt 1 tablespoon (15 mL) butter in non-stick skillet over medium heat.
4. Fry bread in skillet, turning once, for 2 to 3 minutes. Repeat with remaining slices, adding more butter as needed.
5. Serve with maple syrup and fresh berries.

# F

## French Toast Sticks

Yield: 4-6

**Ingredients:**

- 8 slices sandwich bread or thick-sliced Texas toast
- 2 tablespoons granulated sugar
- 2 medium-large eggs
- 1 cup milk half and half, coconut milk, or almond milk
- 1 teaspoon vanilla extract
- 1 teaspoon ground cinnamon
- pinch salt
- butter
- maple syrup

**Method:**

1. First, whisk together eggs, milk, salt, vanilla, and cinnamon in a flat-bottomed pie plate or baking dish.
2. Cut bread into thirds and place a few at a time into the egg mixture and flip to make sure both sides of bread are well-coated.
3. Add granulated sugar to a shallow plate. Remove dipped French toast sticks from the wet batter and place in the plate of granulated sugar and lightly coat both sides of the sticks.
4. Melt butter in a large skillet or on a griddle.

5. Place bread sticks in skillet or on griddle and cook until golden browned on each side and crisp, about 3-5 minutes.
6. Serve immediately or keep warm in oven until ready to serve, but no longer than about 30 minutes.

*To freeze for later use:*

1. Place cooked French toast sticks on a baking sheet pan and freeze until firm, about 30 - 45 minutes. Transfer to a freezer-safe airtight container or freezer-safe zip top bag and store in the freezer.
2. When ready to reheat, preheat oven to 425° F, remove the number of French toast sticks desired from the freezer and place onto a rimmed baking sheet pan in the oven and bake for about 12-15 minutes, until heated throughout.
3. Serve with Maple Syrup.

# French Toast with Smoked Salmon and Crème Fraiche

Serves: 4

## Ingredients:

- 250ml milk
- 4 thick slices of brioche or sandwich bread
- 4 tablespoons crème fraiche
- 1 tablespoon of butter
- 1 free range egg
- 1 tablespoon maille originale mustard
- 1 tablespoon dill (chopped)
- smoked salmon
- zest of 1 lemon
- salt and pepper
- lemon wedges

## Method:

1. First, whisk the egg and milk together with a pinch of salt, then gently stir in the mustard.
2. Transfer to a large shallow dish and place the brioche in the egg mixture, soak for a minute on each side.
3. Combine the crème fraiche, dill, lemon zest and a good grind of fresh black pepper and set aside.
4. Heat the butter in a large frying pan on a medium heat. Add the brioche and cook for 2-3 minutes or until golden, then flip the slices over and cook the other side.
5. Serve with a dollop of crème fraiche, a couple of ribbons of smoked salmon and lemon wedges.

# French Toast Cupcakes

Yield: 1 ½ dozen

## Ingredients:

- 2 medium-large eggs
- 2 teaspoons vanilla extract
- 2 cups all-purpose flour
- 2 teaspoons ground cinnamon
- 1 ½ cups sugar
- 1 1/3 cups buttermilk
- ½ cup butter (softened)
- ½ teaspoon baking powder
- ½ teaspoon baking soda
- ¼ teaspoon salt
- ¼ teaspoon ground nutmeg

*Maple buttercream frosting:*

- 2 ½ cups confectioners' sugar
- ½ cup maple syrup
- ½ cup butter, softened
- ¼ cup shortening
- dash salt
- 6 bacon strips (cooked and crumbled, optional)

## Method:

1. Cream butter and sugar in a large bowl until light and fluffy.
2. Add eggs, one at a time, beating well after each addition. Beat in vanilla. Combine the flour, cinnamon, baking powder, baking soda, salt and

nutmeg; add to the creamed mixture alternately with buttermilk, beating well after each addition.

3. Fill paper-lined muffin cups two-thirds full. Bake at 350° for 17-22 minutes or until a toothpick inserted in the center comes out clean.

4. Cool for 10 minutes before removing from pans to wire racks to cool completely.

*For frosting:*

1. In a small bowl, beat butter and shortening until fluffy. Beat in maple syrup and salt. Add confectioners' sugar; beat until smooth. Frost cupcakes. Sprinkle with bacon if desired.

# French Toast Lasagna

Servings: 4-6

## Ingredients:

- ½ pound thin sliced deli ham
- 2 packages (12-½ ounces each) frozen French toast
- 2 cups shredded three-cheese blend (divided)
- 1 can (21 ounces) apple pie filling
- 1 cup granola with raisins
- 1 cup sour cream
- 1/3 cup packed brown sugar

## Method:

1. First, combine sour cream and brown sugar in a small bowl; refrigerate until serving.
2. In a greased 13x9-in. baking dish, layer six slices French toast, ham, 1-1/2 cups cheese and remaining French toast.
3. Spread with pie filling and sprinkle with granola. Bake, uncovered, at 350° for 25 minutes. Top with remaining cheese. Bake 5 minutes longer or until cheese is melted.
4. Serve with sour cream mixture.

# Fattiga Riddare (Swedish Poor Knights French Toast)

Servings: 4

## Ingredients:

- 1 loaf white bread
- 800 ml milk
- 225 g flour (around 400 ml)
- 4 medium-large eggs
- 1 teaspoon ground ginger optional
- 1 teaspoon cardamom optional
- ½ teaspoon salt

## Method:

1. Start by mixing the dry ingredients in a bowl.
2. Use a hand mixer and add around ½ of the milk. This way you will be able to avoid lumps of flour in the batter.
3. Once the batter is evenly mixed then add the rest of the milk and then add the eggs.
4. Add the same amount of bread slices you can fit in your pan to the pancake batter and let it soak a few minutes (how long depends on the bread).
5. Fry the soaked breads in some butter until they have a nice golden brown on each side.
6. At the same time, you start frying, you should add some more bread slices to the batter for soaking while you fry.
7. Serve hot with same topping as you would with pancakes. The typical Swedish topping is strawberry jam and whipped cream, but any jam would do.

Lemon juice with sugar is also quite popular. Or just fresh fruits or berries.

# G

## Golden Brioche French Toast

Servings: 2-4

**Ingredients:**

- 1 loaf of brioche (sliced thick)
- 3 medium-large eggs
- 3 tablespoons of cane sugar or lightly packed brown sugar
- 2 tablespoons salted butter (melted)
- 2 tablespoons salted butter or grapeseed oil (for frying)
- 1 ½ teaspoon cinnamon (ground)
- 1 pint of heavy whipping cream or milk (warmed)
- 1 tablespoon of vanilla extract (vary it with almond extract)

**Method:**

1. First, whisk eggs, milk, sugar, vanilla (or almond) extract, cinnamon and two tablespoons of melted butter.
2. Soak bread, both sides till saturated but not falling apart.
3. In a 12-inch skillet, heat remaining butter over medium low heat.
4. Carefully place slices of bread in the pan to fit. When the side gets golden brown, flip until second side is golden brown. Continue cooking till all the slices of bread is done.

5. Cool and then put in an airtight container or Ziplock bag and freeze.
6. To reheat, just place a slice on a plate and heat for 40 seconds.

# Golden Bread (Canadian French Toast)

Yield: 3-6 servings

## Ingredients:

- 6 slices bread (day old)
- 3 tablespoons butter
- 3 medium-large eggs
- 1 tablespoon sugar
- 1 cup milk
- ½ teaspoon vanilla extract
- ¼ teaspoon cinnamon
- maple syrup (garnish)

## Method:

1. First, beat the eggs, sugar, vanilla extract, and cinnamon together until the mixture is completely blended and smooth.
2. Stir the milk into the egg mixture until it is fully incorporated. Place the slices of bread into the egg mixture, turn them over to coat all the surfaces, and allow the bread to soak for 5 minutes.
3. Melt 1 tablespoon butter in a large skillet set over medium heat.
4. Cook 2 slices of soaked bread in the melted butter for 3 minutes. Turn the slices of French toast over and cook them for an additional 3 minutes, until they are golden brown and lightly crispy on each side.
5. Repeat with the remaining butter and soaked bread.
6. Serve with maple syrup.

# Gingerbread French Toast with Cinnamon Honey Sauce

Yield: 12 toasts

## Ingredients:

*For the French Toast:*

- 12 slices French baguette (2.5cm/1inch thick, a day or two old)
- 3 tablespoons (50g) unsalted butter (for frying)
- 2 medium-large eggs
- 1 teaspoon mixed spices (ground cinnamon, star anise, cloves or ginger)
- ¼ cup (60ml) heavy cream
- ¼ cup (60ml) milk

*For the Cinnamon Honey Sauce/Dip:*

- 5 tablespoons honey
- 3 tablespoons (50g) unsalted butter (heaped)
- 2 tablespoons (30ml) lemon juice (freshly squeezed)
- 1 teaspoon cinnamon
- ¼ cup (60ml) heavy cream

## Method:

1. Whisk the eggs, milk, cream and spices in a mixing bowl or an oven dish until well combined.
2. Slice the baguette into 2.5cm (1inch) slices.
3. Melt butter in a frying pan. Dip each bread slice in the batter and add them to the pan. Cook until nice golden. This will take about 1-2 minutes. Flip each

bread slice over and cook for a further 1-2 minutes or until golden.

4. *For the Cinnamon Honey Dip,* you simply melt butter in a saucepan. Add cinnamon, honey and lemon juice. Stir until well combined. Slowly pour in the cream while stirring constantly. Slowly bring to a boil and stir for a further minute.

5. Pour over the toast or dip each French toast in and enjoy!

# Gluten-Free French Toast

Serves: 2

## Ingredients:

- 4 slices of your favorite gluten-free bread (mountain white, 7-grain or cinnamon raisin)
- 2 large eggs
- splash of cream or milk
- splash of vanilla

## Method:

1. First, whisk eggs with cream (or milk) and vanilla in a bowl.
2. Dip each piece of bread in the egg mixture to coat. Let it soak in well, so you don't have any egg left over.
3. Fry in coconut oil until golden brown on both sides.
4. Serve with butter, seasonal fruit and whipped cream or your favorite French toast topping!

# H

## Herb French Toast

Yield: 6 pieces

### Ingredients:

- 6 slices French bread, sliced on a bias (into 1-inch thick pieces)
- 5 medium-large eggs
- 2 tablespoons whole grain mustard
- 2 teaspoons chives (thinly sliced)
- 2 teaspoons thyme (minced)
- 1 ½ teaspoons salt
- 1 cup whole milk
- 1 teaspoon oregano (minced)
- 1 garlic clove (minced)
- 1 teaspoon coriander (ground)
- 1 teaspoon dry mustard
- ½ teaspoon black pepper (cracked)
- ½ cup (1 stick) unsalted butter (divided)
- fried eggs (cooked to your liking)
- microgreens

### Method:

1. First, place eggs, milk, mustard, herbs, garlic, spices, salt, and pepper into a shallow baking dish and whisk together.
2. Place a large skillet over medium heat, add 4 tablespoons butter and melt. Press 3 slices bread

into the egg mixture to soak. Flip each slice and soak for about 1 minute.

3. Carefully transfer soaked bread slices to the hot skillet and sear for 3 to 4 minutes or until nicely browned. Flip each slice and continue to cook until browned and French toast has cooked through, an additional 3 to 4 minutes.

4. Remove the French toast slices from the pan and repeat steps 2 and 3 with the remaining bread slices.

5. Top each serving of French toast with a fried egg, sprinkle of salt and pepper and fresh micro greens.

6. Serve.

# Hong Kong-style French toast

Serves: 4

**Ingredients:**

- 1 cup (280g) crunchy peanut butter
- 8 x 2cm-thick slices white bread
- 4 medium-large eggs (lightly beaten)
- 1 teaspoon vanilla bean paste
- sunflower oil (to shallow-fry eggs)
- maple syrup and condensed milk (to serve)

**Method:**

1. First, spread peanut butter on one side of all the bread slices.
2. Sandwich slices of bread, peanut-butter side in between, to make 4 sandwiches.
3. Heat 2cm oil in a heavy-based frypan over medium heat until it reaches 160°C (a cube of bread will turn golden in 45 seconds when oil is hot enough).
4. Whisk eggs and vanilla paste in a bowl. Soak sandwiches in egg mixture, turning, until thoroughly coated.
5. In batches, cook egg-soaked sandwiches for 4 minutes each side or until golden.
6. Drain on paper towel. Repeat with remaining sandwiches.
7. Slice the French toast into triangles, then serve stacked and drizzled with maple syrup and condensed milk.

# I

## Irish Cream French Toast

Serves: 4

### Ingredients:

- 1 loaf French bread or 1 loaf challah (sliced ¾-inch thick)
- 4 large eggs
- 2 cups half-and-half
- ½ cup Irish cream (Irish Cream Liqueur)
- ¼ cup butter

### Method:

1. First, preheat an iron skillet over medium-low heat.
2. Whisk the eggs in a medium-sized bowl until they are well-blended.
3. Add the Irish cream and half-and-half and whisk together.
4. Soak the slices of bread in the egg mixture; turn the slices to ensure that they are well-coated.
5. Place 2 tablespoons of butter in skillet and allow to melt.
6. Place soaked slices of bread in pan and cook until golden on each side.
7. Continue to repeat process until all of the egg mixture has been used.
8. Serve immediately with warm maple syrup and fresh seasonal fruits.

# J

## Japanese French Toast

Servings: 1

### Ingredients:

- 30 grams salmon flakes
- 10 grams mayonnaise with mustard
- 2 teaspoons milk
- 2 medium-large eggs (whisked)
- 2 slices bread
- 1 sheet nori
- 1 slice cheese
- 1 tablespoon dashi stock

### Method:

1. First, spread mayonnaise with mustard onto bread. Then top with nori, salmon flakes, cheese and another slice of bread.
2. Combine whisked egg, milk and dashi stock into a tray and soak bread in mixture.
3. Cook both sides in a frying pan until golden brown.
4. Cut in half and transfer to a plate.
5. Wrap nori sheet around each and enjoy.

# K

## Krachel French Toast

Serves: 6-8

**Ingredients:**

- 120 ml whole milk
- 8 krachel
- 4 tablespoons caster sugar
- 3 large eggs
- 1 teaspoon vanilla extract
- ½ teaspoon ground cinnamon
- ½ teaspoon ras el hanout
- pinch salt
- maple syrup to serve
- strawberries and peaches (sliced, to serve)

**Method:**

1. First, beat together the milk, eggs, sugar, vanilla extract, cinnamon, ras el hanout and salt in a large shallow dish (such as a pie plate).
2. Halve the krachel, dip each half in the egg mixture and soak for 3 minutes on each side.
3. Melt the butter in a frying pan over medium heat and fry the krachel halves until golden brown, about 3 minutes on each side.
4. Serve with maple syrup, sliced strawberries and peaches.

# L

## Lemon French Toast with Poached Plums

Serves: 4

### Ingredients:

- 450g plums (halved and stoned)
- 100ml milk
- 50g butter
- 4 tablespoons caster sugar
- 4 slices bread or brioche (cut in half diagonally)
- 2 large eggs (beaten)
- 1 tablespoon lemon juice
- zest 1 lemon
- crème fraîche or vanilla ice cream (to serve)

### Method:

1. Start by mixing the eggs, milk, lemon zest and 1 tablespoon sugar in a shallow dish. Add the bread, then turn in the liquid until well soaked.
2. Put 2 tablespoons sugar and 25g butter in a frying pan, then heat gently until the sugar has melted.
3. Add the plums, then fry until they are softened and the juice is golden brown, about 5 mins. Add the lemon juice, then heat gently to make a light syrup.
4. Heat the remaining butter in a large non- stick frying pan, then add the slices of bread and fry on each side until golden brown.

5. Put two slices on each plate, sprinkle with the remaining sugar, then spoon over the plums and their juices.
6. Serve as they are or with crème fraîche or vanilla ice cream.

# M

## Marmalade-Stuffed French Toast with Orange Syrup

Yield: 4 servings

### Ingredients:

- 8 2 1/2 x 4 1/2-inch slices French bread (each about 1 inch thick)
- 4 ounces cream cheese (room temperature)
- 4 medium-large eggs
- 2 tablespoons (¼ stick) butter
- 1 cup milk
- 1 teaspoon vanilla extract
- ¼ cup marmalade
- ¼ teaspoon ground cinnamon
- 1/8 teaspoon ground nutmeg
- orange syrup

### Method:

1. First, preheat oven to 300° F.
2. Place baking sheet in oven. Cutting through top crust of each bread slice, make 4-inch-long by 2-inch-deep pocket.
3. Stir cream cheese and marmalade in small bowl. Spoon 1 generous tablespoonful cream cheese mixture into each bread pocket.
4. Whisk eggs, milk, vanilla extract, cinnamon and nutmeg in pie plate.

5. Dip 4 stuffed bread slices into egg mixture, coating completely.
6. Melt 1 tablespoon butter in large nonstick skillet over medium heat. Add dipped bread to skillet. Cook until golden brown, about 2 minutes per side.
7. Transfer French toast to baking sheet in oven. Repeat dipping and cooking with remaining 4 bread slices, egg mixture and 1 tablespoon butter.
8. Serve with orange syrup.

# Monte Cristo Sandwich (Ham Cheese French Toast)

Servings: 2

## Ingredients:

- 4 slices bread of choice *(see note)*
- 2-4 slices gruyere cheese (or other grated or sliced melting cheese of choice)
- 2 teaspoons mayonnaise
- 1 - 2 tablespoons unsalted butter
- 1 large egg or 2 small eggs
- 1 tablespoon milk
- salt
- ham or turkey (sliced or shaved)

## Method:

1. Start by lightly whisking egg, milk and a generous pinch of salt in a flat bowl.
2. Spread 2 slices of bread with mayonnaise.
3. Top with ham, then cheese, then sandwich with remaining slices of bread. Press down firmly.
4. Melt butter in a skillet over medium heat.
5. Dip each side of the sandwiches briefly in the egg mixture, then place in skillet.
6. Cook the first side, pressing down with an egg flip, for 3 minutes or until deep golden brown.
7. Flip and cook the other side for 3 minutes, pressing down firmly with the egg flip, until golden brown and the cheese is melted.
8. Serve immediately, while hot!

*Note:*

- This is great made with artisan (e.g. sourdough) bread or ordinary sandwich bread. Sourdough yields a slightly crunchier golden crust whereas sandwich bread has a higher ratio of soft gooey melted cheese and hot ham.

# N

## Nutella Stuffed French Toast

Yield: 2

### Ingredients:

- 4-6 tablespoons Nutella
- 4 slices French bread
- 2 tablespoons butter
- 2 medium-large eggs
- ½ cup caramel syrup or your favorite syrup (for serving)
- ¼ cup milk
- powdered sugar (for serving)

### Method:

1. First, whisk the eggs and milk together in a shallow bowl or pie plate.
2. Spread 2 slices of the bread with the Nutella, about 2-3 tablespoons per slice. Place the other slices of bread on top and gently press them together. Carefully dip both sides of each sandwich into the egg mixture until well coated.
3. In a large skillet, melt the butter.
4. Add the French toast sandwiches and cook until golden, about 4 minutes per side.
5. Cut the sandwiches in half on the diagonal and transfer to plates.
6. Drizzle with syrup and dust with powdered sugar and serve immediately.

# O

## One-Dish Blackberry French Toast

Yield: 8-10 servings

### Ingredients:

- 4 medium-large eggs
- 2 cups half-and-half
- 1 (12-oz.) French bread loaf (cut into 1 ½-inch cubes)
- 1 (8-oz.) package 1/3-less-fat cream cheese (cut into 1-inch cubes)
- 1 cup blackberry jam
- 1 teaspoon ground cinnamon
- 1 teaspoon vanilla extract
- ½ cup firmly packed brown sugar
- maple syrup, whipped cream (toppings)

### Method:

1. Start by cooking the jam in a small saucepan over medium heat 1 to 2 minutes or until melted and smooth, stirring once.
2. Place half of bread cubes in bottom of a lightly greased 13- x 9-inch baking dish. Top with cream cheese cubes, and drizzle with melted jam. Top with remaining bread cubes.
3. Whisk together eggs and next 3 ingredients. Pour over bread mixture. Sprinkle with brown sugar. Cover tightly, and chill 8 to 24 hours.

4. Preheat oven to 325°. Bake, covered, 20 minutes. Uncover and bake 10 to 15 minutes or until bread is golden brown and mixture is set.
5. Serve with desired toppings.

# Onion Soup French Toast

Yield: 4

## Ingredients:

- 1 loaf of brioche, about 400gr
- 250gr emmental or gruyere cheese (thinly sliced or shredded)

*For the onions:*

- 7 medium white onions (thinly sliced)
- 5 sprigs of thyme (leaves only)
- 2 tablespoons of butter (plus extra for frying the French toast)
- 1 shot of port
- 1 shot of white wine
- salt and pepper to taste

*For the egg batter:*

- 250ml of cream
- 3 cups of milk
- 3 medium eggs
- salt

## Method:

1. Start by melting the butter in a large pan over medium heat. Add the sliced onions, thyme, salt and pepper. Cook for about 10 minutes, stirring from time to time.
2. After the 10 minutes have passed and the onions are caramelized, add the port and white wine to

deglaze the pan. Stir, so nothing is stuck to the bottom of the pan.

3. Once the liquid has evaporated, turn the heat off and transfer the onions to a plate.

4. Slice the brioche loaf into thick slices of about 5 or 6cm. The slices need to be big in order to be able to hold the filling. Using a paring knife, cut through the top part of the crust of each slice to create a pocket.

5. Stuff each slice with some of the caramelized onions and cheese. Then using your fingers, press together the opening of each toast to seal it and keep the stuffing from coming out while cooking.

6. Mix the egg batter with a whisk in a large bowl.

7. In a large pan, add about 2 tablespoons of butter and melt it over low heat.

8. Soak 2 of the stuffed pieces of bread in the egg batter. Then place them on the pan and cook for about 4 to 5 minutes on each side on low heat. Then repeat for the remaining pieces.

9. Serve right away.

# P

## Praline French Toast

Yield: about 9 servings

**Ingredients:**

*Glaze:*

- 2 tablespoons honey, maple syrup or corn syrup
- 1 cup brown sugar
- ½ cup (8 tablespoons) butter

*Bread:*

- French or Italian bread sliced ½" thick, enough to cover the bottom of a 9" x 13" pan

*Custard:*

- 5 medium-large eggs, or 1 ¼ cups egg substitute
- 1 ½ cups whipping cream, half and half, milk, or fat-free half and half
- ½ teaspoon flavor: pralines & cream, eggnog, vanilla-butternut, or your choice; OR 2 teaspoons vanilla extract
- ¼ teaspoon salt

*Topping:*

- ½ cup brown sugar
- ¼ teaspoon ground cinnamon
- ¼ teaspoon ground nutmeg

**Method:**

1. Start by lightly greasing a 9" x 13" pan or shallow 2-quart casserole.

*To make the glaze:*

1. Melt the butter in a saucepan and stir in the brown sugar and syrup. Bring the mixture to a simmer, cooking until the sugar melts. Pour the glaze into the prepared pan, spreading it to the corners.
2. Lay the slices of bread in the pan, atop the glaze. Use baguettes for smaller servings, a fat loaf of Italian bread for larger servings. Leftover/stale bread works well here; kids may prefer softer, sandwich-type bread, which will make softer, smoother French toast. Adults seem to prefer bread with more body.

*To make the custard:*

1. Whisk together the cream, half and half, or milk, eggs or egg substitute, the flavor, and the salt. Pour it over the bread in the pan, pressing the bread down into the custard.
3. Cover the pan, and refrigerate overnight, or for up to 24 hours.
4. When you're ready to bake, preheat the oven to 350°F.
5. Make the topping by stirring together the brown sugar, nutmeg, and cinnamon. Sprinkle it evenly over the bread.
6. Bake the French toast for 40 to 45 minutes, until it's bubbly and the top is very lightly browned.

7. Remove it from the oven, and allow it to cool for 10 to 15 minutes before serving. Serve individual slices of bread, turning it over on the plate so the syrupy bottom is on top.

*Notes:*

- This can also be made as bread pudding. Simply cut or tear leftover bread into 1/2" pieces, and arrange pieces one layer deep, tightly packed, in the pan.
- The recipe as written makes a very sweet French toast. Omit or reduce the brown sugar sprinkled on top just before baking, if desired.

# Pumpkin Spice French Toast

Yield: 10 slices

**Ingredients:**

- 10 slices thick bread (such as Texas toast or challah)
- 4 medium-large eggs
- 2 tablespoons light brown sugar
- 2 teaspoons pumpkin pie spice
- 1 teaspoon vanilla extract
- ¾ cup milk (any kind)
- ½ cup pure pumpkin
- ½ teaspoon cinnamon
- butter for skillet

**Method:**

1. First, preheat electric griddle or non-stick skillet over medium heat. Set aside.
2. Whisk eggs, milk, pumpkin, light brown sugar, vanilla extract, pumpkin pie spice, and cinnamon in a large bowl. Pour into a shallow baking dish to dip the bread, if needed.
3. Dip bread into egg mixture and lightly press down to coat both sides.
4. Melt butter in skillet. Transfer bread to skillet and cook on each side for 3-4 minutes, or until golden brown. Repeat with rest of bread slices.
5. Serve immediately with powdered sugar, butter, and/or maple syrup, if desired.

# Pain Perdu (Real French Toast)

Yield: 2 slices

## Ingredients:

*For custard:*

- 3 tablespoons granulated sugar
- 2 medium-large eggs
- 1 tablespoon armagnac
- 1 teaspoon vanilla extract
- ½ cup whole milk
- ½ cup heavy cream

*For pain perdu:*

- 2 slices batard (sliced 2-inches thick)
- 2 tablespoons cultured unsalted butter
- 1 tablespoon superfine sugar
- 1 tablespoon all-purpose flour

## Method:

1. Start by making the custard for the Pain Perdu but whisk together the milk, heavy cream, eggs, sugar, Armagnac, and vanilla extract until the mixture is completely homogenous.
2. Place the bread in in a deep dish or tray that is just large enough to hold the bread in a single layer and cover with the custard. If your dish is too large the custard won't soak into the bread completely.
3. If you don't have a suitable dish, you can use a sealable plastic bag and press out the excess air.

Cover and refrigerate for a day, turning the bread over a few times in between.

4. Preheat the oven to 450 F (230 C). Remove the soaked Pain Perdu from the refrigerator and flip one more time.

5. Mix 1 tablespoon of sugar with 1 tablespoon of flour and sprinkle half the mixture onto the tops of the bread using a small sieve (such as a tea strainer) to ensure the flour gets sprinkled evenly.

6. Add the butter to a cast-iron skillet and heat over medium heat.

7. When the butter has melted and the foaming subsides, add the bread with flour-sprinkled side down.

8. Dust the Pain Perdu with the remaining flour/sugar mixture and fry until it's well browned on one side (about 5 minutes). If your heat is up too high it will burn, so if it looks like it's browning too quickly, turn the heat down.

9. Flip the bread over and put the pan in the oven.

10. Bake for 8-10 minutes. Keep a close eye on it as the sugar will burn easily. You want the surface of your Pain Perdu to be very dark, but not burnt.

11. Serve and enjoy.

# Parmesan French Toast with Hollandaise Sauce

Serves: 4-6

## Ingredients:

*For the French toast:*

- 4 medium-large eggs
- 1 medium-large garlic clove (crushed)
- ½ cup whole milk
- ½ cup heavy cream
- ½ cup grated parmesan (plus more for garnish)
- ½ teaspoon dry mustard powder
- ½ teaspoon hot sauce
- salt and pepper to taste
- medium-size loaf of good-quality bread (cut 1-inch thick)
- butter (for frying)
- flat-leaf parsley or chives (for garnish)

*For the hollandaise:*

- 3 egg yolks
- 1 tablespoon lemon juice
- 1 dash hot sauce
- ½ cup butter
- ¼ teaspoon Dijon mustard

## Method:

*For the French toast:*

1. First, turn your oven on to the warm setting (170 F). Set a cooling rack over a cookie sheet and place in the oven.
2. Add eggs, milk, cream, Parmesan, mustard powder, hot sauce, black pepper, garlic, and salt to a blender. Blend until smooth. Pour liquid into a pie plate or an 8x8 dish. Rinse out your blender immediately.
3. Slice the bread into 1-inch pieces.
4. Heat a griddle or a large skillet to medium-high heat.
5. Soak the bread in the egg mixture 1-2 minutes each side.
6. Grease the griddle or pan with butter.
7. Fry each piece of bread for about 2-3 minutes, until golden brown. Flip and cook the other side for 1-2 minutes or until browned. Continue with all the bread pieces, replenishing butter as necessary.
8. Place each finished piece of toast on the cooling rack in the oven.

*For the hollandaise:*

1. In the rinsed-out blender, add the egg yolks, Dijon mustard, lemon juice, and hot sauce. Blend until smooth.
2. In a small bowl in the microwave, melt butter completely so that it's very hot.
3. Open the top spout of your blender. Turn the blender on low and pour in the hot butter. It should thicken immediately.
4. Immediately pour the sauce into a measuring cup or bowl. Place the bowl into another bowl of very hot

water. (You want to keep the sauce hot, but if you microwave it, it will curdle.)

5. Pour the sauce over each serving. Whisk the sauce if it starts to separate.
6. Top each French toast with fresh herbs and extra Parmesan.

# Puffy French Toast

Yield: 12 slices

## Ingredients:

- 12 slices Texas style toast (cut in half diagonally)
- 2 ½ teaspoon baking powder
- 2 ½ tablespoons sugar
- 2 medium-large eggs
- 1 ½ cups milk
- 1 cup flour
- ½ teaspoon salt
- ½ teaspoon vanilla extract
- cinnamon sugar

## Method:

1. First, in a large skillet or frying pan, heat about ¼″ of vegetable oil (not olive oil) over medium heat.
2. Whisk together eggs, sugar, salt, vanilla, milk, flour, and baking powder in a shallow bowl or pie plate.
3. Working quickly, take each ½ slice of bread and soak it both sides in the milk/egg/flour mixture. If you leave it in too long, it will get soggy, but you want to make sure enough of the egg mixture has soaked into the bread.
4. Gently shake to remove excess batter and place in hot oil.
5. Cook until puffed, golden brown, and a nice, crispy crust has formed on each side (about 3-5 minutes per side; you really need to babysit them and make sure they're cooking correctly) and then remove from oil and drain on a paper towel.

6. When ready to serve, roll each piece in cinnamon sugar.

# Pecan Upside-Down French Toast Casserole

Yield: 8-10

**Ingredients:**

- 1 (1-pound loaf) French bread (cut in 1-inch slices, then cut in half)
- 6 medium-large eggs
- 3 tablespoons sugar
- 2 teaspoons grated orange zest
- 2 navel oranges squeezed (about 1 cup)
- 2 tablespoons maple syrup
- 1 teaspoon cinnamon
- 1 teaspoon vanilla extract
- 1 cup brown sugar (packed)
- ½ cup pecans (chopped)
- ½ cup nonfat milk
- 1/3 cup butter (melted)

**Method:**

1. First, butter a 9 x 13-inch pan and sprinkle the brown sugar over the bottom.
2. Combine melted butter and maple syrup; stir into brown sugar, spreading mixture evenly over bottom of the pan. Sprinkle with the chopped pecans.
3. In a medium bowl, whisk together orange zest, orange juice, milk, sugar, cinnamon, vanilla and eggs.
4. Pack bread pieces into dish crust side down. Pour egg mixture over bread. Cover and refrigerate overnight.

5. Preheat oven to 350 F. Remove dish from the fridge and turn bread slices over to absorb any excess egg mixture.
6. Bake for 30 to 35 minutes until lightly browned and edges are bubbly.
7. To serve, cut into squares with a spatula and invert so the pecans are on top.

# Panettone French Toast

Yield: 4-6 servings

## Ingredients:

*Syrup:*

- 1 cup water
- 1 packed cup brown sugar
- 2 tablespoons whipping cream
- 1/2 teaspoon ground cinnamon

*French toast:*

- 1 (1-pound) panettone (paper removed)
- 6 large eggs
- 2 tablespoons unsalted butter (divided)
- ¾ cup heavy whipping cream
- ¾ cup whole milk
- ½ cup mascarpone cheese
- ¼ cup sugar
- Serving suggestion: powdered sugar and assorted fresh berries.

## Method:

For the syrup:

1. First, bring the water and sugar to a boil in a medium saucepan over high heat, stirring until the sugar dissolves. Boil until the syrup reduces to 1 cup, about 10 minutes.
2. Remove the pan from the heat and whisk in the cream and cinnamon. Keep the syrup warm over

low heat until ready to serve. (The syrup can be made 1 day ahead. Cool, then cover and refrigerate. Reheat before serving).

For the French toast:

1. Preheat the oven to 200 F. Preheat a nonstick griddle or large nonstick sauté pan over medium heat.
2. Remove the top from the panettone using a serrated knife. Cut the bottom of the panettone in half crosswise. Cut each half into 4 equal pieces.
3. In a large bowl, whisk together the eggs, cream, milk, and sugar until smooth. Melt 1 tablespoon of butter on the griddle. Working in batches, dip slices of panettone into the custard, turning to allow both sides to absorb the custard. Cook the soaked panettone slices until golden brown and firm to the touch, about 4 minutes per side.
4. Transfer the French toast to a baking sheet and keep warm in the oven. Repeat with remaining 1 tablespoon butter and panettone slices.
5. Transfer the French toast to plates. Drizzle the cinnamon syrup over the French toast and place a dollop of mascarpone on top.
6. Lightly dust with powdered sugar and serve with fresh berries.

# Peanut Butter and Jelly French Toast

Serves: 4

## Ingredients:

- 8 slices bread
- 4 tablespoons jelly or 4 tablespoons jam
- 2 medium-large eggs
- 2 tablespoons butter or 2 tablespoons margarine
- ½ cup peanut butter
- ½ cup milk
- 1/8 teaspoon salt

## Method:

1. Start by spreading peanut butter on 4 slices of bread; spread jelly on other 4 slices of bread.
2. Put one slice of each together to form sandwiches.
3. In mixing bowl, lightly beat eggs; add milk and salt and mix together.
4. Melt butter in a large skillet over medium heat.
5. Dip sandwiches in egg mixture, coating well.
6. Place in skillet and brown both sides.
7. Serve immediately.

# Piña Colada French Toast

Serves: 4

## Ingredients:

- 8 slices ciabatta bread
- 6 tablespoons coconut oil
- ½ cup unsweetened, shaved coconut for toasting (optional)

*Finely ground coconut:*

- 2 cups unsweetened coconut (shredded)

*For the dipping mixture:*

- 5 tablespoons butter (melted and cooled)
- 4 tablespoons sugar
- 4 teaspoons vanilla
- 2 medium-large eggs
- 1 ½ cups coconut milk

*For the dredging mixture:*

- 2 tablespoons brown sugar
- 1 cup unsweetened coconut (shredded)

*For the glaze:*

- 4 tablespoons butter (melted)
- 1 ½ cups powdered sugar
- 1 tablespoon dark rum
- ½ cup pineapple juice

*For the coconut whipped cream:*

- 4 tablespoons powdered sugar
- 1 ½ cups heavy cream
- ½ cup coconut milk

## Method:

1. First, place two cups of shredded, unsweetened coconut in a blender or the bowl of a food processor and finely grind the coconut until it is the texture of sand. You will use half of this ground coconut in the dipping mixture and the other half in the dredging mixture.

*To make the dipping mixture:*

1. In a medium bowl, combine butter, coconut milk, 1/2 of the finely ground shredded coconut, sugar, vanilla and eggs. Beat until well combined.
2. Transfer dipping mixture to a shallow dish and set aside.

*To make the dredging mixture:*

1. In a small bowl, combine the remaining finely ground shredded coconut, 1 cup unsweetened shredded coconut flakes and brown sugar. Stir to combine. Transfer to a shallow dish and set aside.

*To make the glaze:*

1. Combine powdered sugar, pineapple juice, melted butter and dark rum in a small bowl and use a beater or immersion blender to whip until frothy and smooth.

*To make the coconut whipped cream:*

1. Combine heavy cream, coconut milk and powdered sugar in a medium bowl or the bowl of a stand mixer. Using a hand mixer or stand mixer, beat on high speed just until stiff peaks form.

*To make the French toast:*

1. Dip one slice of bread in dipping mixture and turn to fully soak through.
2. Place the dipped bread in the dredging mixture and coat both sides of the bread.
3. Transfer the bread to a 350°, griddle greased with coconut oil. Allow the bread to cook for 4-6 minutes on each side, or until golden brown.
4. Remove bread from griddle. Drizzle with glaze and top with whipped cream. Sprinkle on toasted coconut, if desired.

# Q

## Quick French Toast in A Mug

Yield: 1 mug

### Ingredients:

- 16- oz mug
- 1 ¼ cups bread cubes preferably stale or small plain croutons
- 1 tablespoon granulated sugar
- 1 medium-large egg
- ½ cup milk
- ¼ teaspoon vanilla extract
- 1/8 teaspoon salt
- 1/8 teaspoon ground cinnamon
- pure maple syrup confectioners' sugar or butter (topping)

### Method:

1. In the mug, use a fork to whisk sugar, salt, cinnamon, egg, milk and vanilla until very well blended.
2. Add bread cubes, stirring and pressing them down into the custard to absorb the liquid. Let stand for at least 15 minutes (so the bread absorbs the liquid). Press bread down with a fork to compact.
3. Microwave on High for 1 ½ to 2 ½ minutes (checking at 1 ½) or until firm to the touch and liquid is absorbed. Top with syrup, sugar or butter if preferred.

*Notes:*

- Add up to 2 tablespoons raisins or chopped dried fruit, or 1 tablespoon miniature semisweet chocolate chips with the bread.
- *Prep Ahead Option:* Whisk the sugar, salt, cinnamon, egg, milk and vanilla in the mug, then add the bread cubes; cover and refrigerate until ready to use.

# R

## Rabanada (Brazilian French Toast)

Servings: 4-5

**Ingredients:**

- 1 loaf, stale French bread, Italian bread, brioche, or challah, sliced 1 inch thick
- 4 medium-large eggs
- 3 cup milk
- 1 tablespoon cinnamon
- ¼ cup sugar
- oil for frying (olive or canola)

**Method:**

1. First, mix the sugar and cinnamon on a large plate until blended, set aside.
2. Place the milk in one shallow bowl and the eggs in another. Lightly beat the eggs.
3. In a medium skillet, heat ½ inch of oil to just before it begins to smoke (350-375F).
4. Working with a few slices at a time, dip the bread in the milk letting it soak in. Then, dip the bread in the beaten egg, coating both sides.
5. Place the soaked bread in the hot oil and fry for 2-3 minutes on each side, or until golden brown. Carefully remove the fried French toast from the hot oil and place on a platter that has been lined with paper towels.
6. Continue with the remaining bread.

7. While the fried French toast is still warm, dip both sides in the plate with cinnamon sugar, and serve.

# S

## Strawberry Stuffed French Toast

Yield: 8 servings

**Ingredients:**

*Strawberry & cream cheese filling:*

- 8 oz cream cheese (softened)
- 1 teaspoon vanilla extract
- 1 cup strawberries (sliced)
- ¾ cup powdered sugar (plus more for topping)
- ¼ cup sour cream
- ¼ cup granulated sugar

*Vanilla cinnamon French toast:*

- 3 medium-large egg
- 1 ½ cup milk
- 1 teaspoon vanilla extract
- 1 teaspoon cinnamon (ground)
- 1 loaf French bread cut into 1-inch slices

**Method:**

*Strawberry & cream cheese filling:*

1. Using a stand mixer (or a hand mixer + large bowl), add softened cream cheese, sour cream, powdered sugar, and vanilla.
2. Beat on low until cream cheese has broken down, then mix on medium high until incorporated, about 2 minutes.

3. Use a spatula to scrap around the sides and bottom, then beat again on medium for 30 seconds. Set filling aside.

*For the strawberries:*

1. Slice them as thin as you are able. If using frozen strawberries, use a paper towel to absorb any extra juice; wet strawberries will cause the French toast pieces slip and be hard to flip while cooking. When strawberries are sliced and ready, place them in a small bowl with ¼ cup sugar. Gently toss strawberries until they are all coated in sugar.

*Vanilla cinnamon French toast:*

1. In a small bowl with a flat bottom (or pro tip: use an aluminum pie tin), whisk together milk, eggs, vanilla, and cinnamon. Make sure cinnamon has fully mixed with the wet ingredients and is not just floating on top, still dry.

*Putting it all together:*

1. Spread a layer of cream cheese filling on one side of sliced French bread. Filling should be spread thin (not globbed on) but still thick enough to thoroughly cover bread.
2. Arrange strawberries in an even layer on top of the cream cheese spread, keeping a ¼ inch gap around the sides of the bread
3. Spread another thin layer of cream cheese on a new slice of French bread, then gently press it to the other slice with the strawberries (like a sandwich).
4. Spray a skillet with cooking spray and warm over medium heat.

5. Dip the French toast into the egg and milk mixture, coating both the top and the bottom.
6. Drop the French toast in the skillet and cook each side until golden brown, about 2-4 minutes per side. To make flipping easier, use a thin spatula to scoop under the French toast and gently press your finger on top to secure it while the toast is flipped. Save time by cooking 2-3 sandwiches at once.
7. Serve immediately with powdered sugar and syrup.

# Slow Cooker French Toast

Serving: 8

## Ingredients:

- 1 loaf French bread (cubed)
- 6 medium-large eggs
- 2 cups milk
- 1 ½ teaspoon cinnamon (divided)
- 1 teaspoon vanilla
- ¾ cup pecans (chopped)
- ½ cup brown sugar (packed)
- ¼ cup butter (room temperature)
- ¼ teaspoon nutmeg

## Method:

1. First, place bread cubes in a large bowl.
2. In a separate bowl, beat together eggs, milk, vanilla, and ½ teaspoon cinnamon.
3. Pour egg mixture over bread; mix well. Cover and refrigerate for at least 4 hours to overnight.
4. Spoon bread mixture into a lightly greased 6-quart slow cooker.
5. In a small bowl, mix together butter, brown sugar, pecans, remaining cinnamon and nutmeg; sprinkle over bread mixture.
6. Cover and cook on low for 4 hours, or on high for 2 hours. Let stand 15-20 minutes before serving.

# Strawberry Cheesecake French Toast

Serves: 2

## Ingredients:

- 4 slices bread

*Egg wash:*

- 4 medium-large eggs
- 1 tablespoon vanilla
- 1 cup (240 mL) milk
- 1 tablespoon cinnamon

*Filling:*

- 4 oz (115 g) cream cheese (warmed, for spreading)
- 2 tablespoons vanilla extract
- 2 tablespoons lemon juice
- 1 ½ cups (225 g) strawberry (diced, divided)
- ⅓ cup sugar
- ¾ cup (180 mL) heavy cream (optional)

*Topping:*

- confectioners' sugar
- maple syrup

## Method:

1. First, whisk eggs, cinnamon, vanilla and milk together in medium-large bowl to create egg wash.
2. mix cream cheese, vanilla, sugar, lemon juice and heavy cream in medium bowl (optional).
3. Take 2 slices of bread and spread mixture on both.

4. Press sliced strawberries on both slices & press together.
5. Dunk in egg wash.
6. Melt butter in a skillet on medium-low heat and cook bread for 2-3 minutes or until crumbs are crispy and bread is more solid.
7. Stack and garnish with strawberries and confectioners' sugar. Add maple syrup to preference.
8. Serve and Enjoy!

# Shiitake Mushroom Stuffed French Toast

Serves: 2

## Ingredients:

- 2 cups shiitake mushrooms (sliced)
- 2 medium-large eggs
- 1 ½ tablespoon butter
- 1 teaspoon mirin
- 1 loaf pan bread sliced into ½-inch thick slices
- ½ teaspoon fish sauce
- ½ cup half and half
- ¼ teaspoon salt
- oil (just enough to cover the pan)
- chives (garnish)

## Method:

1. First, heat a skillet over medium heat, add the butter, and sauté the shiitake mushrooms until golden brown.
2. Deglaze the pan with mirin and fish sauce and add the salt. Set aside.
3. Mix, using a fork, the half and half and eggs in a pie pan. Take a slice of the bread and make a small incision into one of the sides of the slices, do not cut all the way through. Stuff some of the mushrooms into each slice of bread.
4. Add oil to a skillet.
5. Dip the slice in the egg and half and half mixture. Soak quickly and ensure coverage on both sides. Place in pan.
6. Brown both sides and maybe even the edges.
7. Plate and garnish with chives.

# Sugar-Crusted French Toast with Honeyed Apples

Servings: 6

**Ingredients:**

*Poached apples:*

- 4 3x1/2-inch strips orange peel
- 4 3x1/2-inch strips lemon peel
- 3 medium apples (peeled, halved, cored)
- 3 cups water
- 2 whole star anise
- 1 cinnamon stick
- ½ vanilla bean (split lengthwise)
- ½ cup honey
- 1/3 cup sugar

*French toast:*

- 6 4x4x1-inch slices egg bread
- 6 tablespoons (¾ stick) unsalted butter
- 6 medium-large eggs
- 3 ½ cups whole milk
- 3 medium-large egg yolks
- 1 tablespoon vanilla extract
- ½ teaspoon salt
- 2/3 cup + 8 tablespoons sugar

**Method:**

*For poached apples:*

1. Combine water, honey, sugar, orange and lemon peel strips, anise and cinnamon stick in heavy large saucepan.
2. Scrape in seeds from vanilla bean; add bean.
3. Bring to boil over medium-high heat, stirring to dissolve sugar. Reduce heat to medium-low; simmer 5 minutes.
4. Add apples; cover and simmer until tender, about 12 minutes. Using slotted spoon, transfer apples to bowl.
5. Boil syrup in saucepan until reduced to 1 ¼ cups, about 10 minutes. Add syrup to bowl with apples. Can be prepared 1 day ahead. Cover and chill. Bring to room temperature before using.

*For french toast:*

1. Whisk eggs, yolks, milk, 2/3 cup sugar, vanilla, and salt in 15x10x2-inch baking dish. Place bread in single layer in egg mixture; spoon egg mixture over bread and let stand until soaked through, about 3 minutes.
2. Melt 3 tablespoons butter in each of 2 large nonstick skillets over medium heat.
3. Sprinkle each skillet with 2 tablespoons sugar.
4. Add 3 bread slices to each skillet; cook until deep golden on bottom, about 3 minutes.
5. Sprinkle top of bread slices with sugar, using 2 tablespoons for each skillet; turn slices over and cook until deep golden on bottom, about 3 minutes.
6. Transfer French toast to plates. Place 1 apple half alongside each serving.
7. Drizzle French toast with some of syrup from apples and serve.
   Sourdough French Toast

## Yield: 4 people, 3 slices each

### Ingredients:

- 12 slices sourdough bread
- 8 tablespoons butter (plus more for serving)
- 4 medium-large eggs
- 3 cups of milk
- 2 teaspoons vanilla
- 1 tablespoon cinnamon
- maple syrup

### Method:

1. First, preheat oven to 200 F.
2. In a 9×13 baking dish, make the batter by combining the milk, eggs, vanilla and cinnamon. Beat to combine.
3. Heat a large nonstick pan over medium high heat. Melt 1 tablespoon of butter in the pan. Dredge the sourdough bread in the batter, turning it 3 times and lightly pressing on the bread so it absorbs the batter.
4. Cook 3 slices of the battered bread in the pan at a time. Flip the bread after the first side is crispy, about 3-4 minutes.
5. Melt another tablespoon of butter in the pan before flipping so the second side also cooks in butter. This will make both sides of the bread crispy. Cook the second side until it is also crispy, another 2-3 minutes.
6. Keep the cooked French toast warm by leaving it in the oven in an oven safe baking dish.
7. Repeat step 3, 4, 5 for the remaining bread.

8. Serve warm with maple syrup and more butter (optional).
9. Will keep an airtight container for 1 week. You can reheat it on the stove in a pan, in the oven, or even in the toaster.

# S'mores French Toast

Servings: 2

## Ingredients:

- 6 large marshmallows (cut in half)
- 3 slices French bread
- 2 medium eggs (lightly beaten)
- 2 full-size Hershey bars (broken into rectangles)
- 1 cup graham cracker crumbs
- 1 teaspoon vanilla extract
- 2/3 cup milk
- ¼ teaspoon salt
- butter
- maple syrup and/or fudge sauce (for serving)

## Method:

1. First, whisk together eggs, milk, vanilla, and salt in a shallow bowl or pie plate.
2. Dip bread into egg mixture, coating each side.
3. Press both sides of bread into graham cracker crumbs.
4. Melt about ½ tablespoon of butter on a griddle or nonstick pan for each slice of bread. Cook until brown and crispy, then flip to other side, adding a little more butter to pan first.
5. While still hot, stack the slices of french toast, layering marshmallows and chocolate in between.
6. Cut in half for 2 servings.

# Streusel Topped French Toast Bake

Servings: 12-14

**Ingredients:**

- 1 loaf stale French bread or challah bread (cut into 1-inch cubes)
- 8 medium-large eggs
- 2 cups milk
- 2 tablespoons vanilla
- 1 teaspoon cinnamon
- ¾ cup sugar
- ½ cup whipping cream
- ½ cup flour
- ½ cup cold butter (cubed)
- ½ cup brown sugar
- ¼ teaspoon salt

**Method:**

1. First, grease or spray (with non-stick spray) a 9x13 baking dish.
2. Place bread pieces in the baking dish.
3. whisk together the eggs, milk, cream, sugar, and vanilla in a large bowl until well blended. Pour evenly over the bread, trying to get every piece wet with the batter.
4. Cover the pan and place in the fridge overnight (at least 8 hours).
5. In another bowl or in your food processor, add the flour, brown sugar, cinnamon, and salt. Mix until blended.

6. Then add the butter cubes and pulse in your food processor or cut with a pastry blender until crumbly with pea sized pieces. Cover streusel mixture and refrigerate.

7. In the morning, preheat oven to 350 F. Uncover the 9 x 13 pan and sprinkle the streusel mixture all over the top.

8. Bake at 350 F for 55 to 60 minutes or until a knife inserted in the center comes out clean.

9. Cut into squares and serve warm topped with maple syrup.

# Sweet Potato French Toast

Servings: 2

## Ingredients:

- 5 cups milk
- 4 slices spelt bread
- 4 cups sweet potato puree
- 4 teaspoons ground cinnamon
- 2 tablespoons unsalted butter
- 2 medium-large eggs
- 1 teaspoon agave nectar or maple syrup
- ground nutmeg (to taste)
- agave nectar or maple syrup (for drizzling)

## Method:

1. Start by melting 1 tablespoon of the butter in a frying pan over medium heat. Cut each slice of bread into four lengthwise sticks.
2. Whisk the sweet potato purée with the eggs, milk and agave nectar. Add the cinnamon and a pinch of nutmeg. Sink each stick from two slices of bread in the egg mixture and flip to coat completely. Place the egg-soaked bread 8 sticks at a time into the hot pan.
3. Cook for 3 mins and then flip. Cook for another 2 mins and remove from the pan.
4. Add the remaining 1 tablespoon of butter to the pan and cook the remaining sticks of bread.
5. Stack and serve warm with maple syrup or agave nectar.

# Sweet and Aromatic French Toast

Servings: 8

## Ingredients:

- 12 thick slices Texas toast
- 3 medium-large eggs
- 2 cups milk
- 1 teaspoon vanilla extract
- 1 tablespoon butter (or as needed)
- ½ cup white sugar
- ½ teaspoon ground cinnamon
- ½ teaspoon ground allspice
- 2 tablespoons confectioners' sugar, or as needed (optional)

## Method:

1. Start by melting butter in a large skillet over medium-high heat.
2. In a large bowl, whisk milk, eggs, sugar, vanilla extract, cinnamon, and allspice together. Dip each slice of bread into egg mixture to coat.
3. Place coated bread into skillet and cook until golden brown on 1 side, about 1 minute. Flip and continue cooking until second side are golden, about 1 minute more. Remove to a plate and repeat with remaining bread slices.
4. Sift confectioners' sugar over top of the French toast, slice diagonally, and serve.

# T

## Tiramisu French Toast

Serves: 12 pancakes

### Ingredients:

- 8 thick slices of bread
- 8 tablespoons butter
- 3 medium-large eggs
- 2 tablespoons maple syrup
- 1 tablespoon amaretto
- 1 teaspoon vanilla extract
- 1 cup milk
- ¼ teaspoon cinnamon
- ¼ teaspoon nutmeg (ground)
- pinch of salt

*Coffee whipped cream topping:*

- 1 teaspoon amaretto
- 1 tablespoon espresso or very strong coffee
- 1 cup cold heavy cream
- 1/3 cup granulated sugar

### Method:

*Prepare the coffee whipped cream:*

1. Whisk the heavy cream and sugar together until stiff peaks form. Gently whisk in the amaretto and espresso. Set the whipped cream into the refrigerator if not using right away.

*For the French toast:*

1. In a flat dish or pie pan, whisk together the eggs, milk, spices, amaretto, maple syrup, vanilla and salt.
2. Preheat a large skillet or cast-iron pan over medium heat. For each slice, melt 1 tablespoon of butter. Soak each slice of bread very well, then drop into hot pan. Toast for 2 to 3 minutes on each side, or until golden brown.
3. Serve immediately with a drizzle of maple syrup, a dollop of coffee whipped cream and a sprinkle of cinnamon.

# Tofu Vegan French Toast

Servings: 6

## Ingredients:

- 8 ounces silken tofu
- 6 slices bread
- 1 teaspoon artificial sweetener (molasses or maple syrup)
- 1 banana
- ½ cup water
- ½ teaspoon cinnamon
- maple syrup
- fresh berries(optional)

## Method:

1. Mix all the ingredients except the bread in a blender until smooth.
2. Pour the mixture into a shallow dish.
3. Dip the bread, and cook on a non-stick pan, turning once when the edges begin to brown.
4. Serve with fresh berries or maple syrup.

# Torrijas (Spanish Style French Toast with Cinnamon and Honey)

Serves: 6

## Ingredients:

- a thick bar of slightly stale French bread (or other, basically what you'd normally use to make a thick French toast)
- 4 medium-large eggs
- 3 tablespoons of honey
- 2 teaspoons of cinnamon
- 1 tablespoon of lemon zest
- 1 teaspoon of cardamom seeds
- 1 liter (about a quart) of whole milk
- 1 cup of sugar
- good quality extra virgin olive oil

## Method:

1. First, bring the liter of milk, ½ cup of sugar, lemon peel, and cardamom seeds to a slow boil.
2. Cut the bread in thick slices.
3. When the milk mixture has been cooking for about 15 minutes, turn off the heat and soak the slices of bread in this mixture. Be careful not to completely wet them to the point that they will break apart, but try to get them to absorb as much milk as possible.
4. Let the slices of wet bread rest and cool (some liquid may be lost).
5. Beat the eggs in a shallow bowl and dip the slices in the egg mixture.

6. In the meantime, heat up about ½ an inch of the olive oil in a deep, heavy pan on a medium high heat.

7. Fry the slices two by two, flipping halfway so that both sides are nice and crisp.

8. Let the French toast rest on paper towels to absorb excess oil. In another bowl mix the remaining sugar (½ cup) with the cinnamon.

9. Cover the slices in the cinnamon sugar mixture and reserve.

10. Finally, make the syrup. Take the remaining cinnamon and sugar from coating the torrijas and add it to a medium sized pot. Add a bit more sugar to completely cover the bottom of the pot if necessary.

11. Add 2 cups of warm water to the sugar and bring it to a boil.

12. Add the honey (you can add more or less depending on preference).

13. Allow the syrup to simmer for about 30 minutes until it reduces to the right consistency. It won't be a very thick syrup, but it shouldn't be too watery.

14. Take the syrup off of the heat and after about 15 minutes spoon it over the French toast. The torrijas should be completely soaked in the syrup. Allow them to completely cool before putting them into the refrigerator.

15. Refrigerate the torrijas at least 4 hours, but preferably overnight.

16. Enjoy within two or three days for best quality.

# Thymey-Wimey French Toast

Servings: 2

## Ingredients:

- 2 thick slices crusty bread
- 2 teaspoons dried thyme leaves
- 1/3 cup sharp cheddar cheese (shredded)
- ¼ cup melted butter
- ¼ cup milk
- salt and pepper to taste

## Method:

1. First, preheat oven to 375 F (190 C).
2. Whisk melted butter and milk together with a fork. Soak the bread slices in the milk mixture, turning to cover both sides completely. Sprinkle half of the thyme over one side of the bread pieces.
3. Heat a dry skillet over medium-low heat, and fry the bread, thyme-side down, until lightly browned, about 5 minutes. Sprinkle the remaining thyme over the bread; turn over and fry until lightly browned, about 5 minutes more.
4. Transfer to a baking sheet; sprinkle with the Cheddar cheese.
5. Bake in the preheated oven until the cheese is bubbly, about 10 minutes.
6. Remove and serve immediately with salt and cracked pepper.

# V

## Vanilla French Toast

Servings: 4

### Ingredients:

- 8 slices dry white or whole wheat bread
- 4 medium-large eggs (lightly beaten)
- 2 tablespoons sugar
- 2 teaspoons vanilla
- 2 tablespoons butter or vegetable oil
- 1 cup half-and-half or light cream
- 1 teaspoon cinnamon (ground)
- ¼ teaspoon nutmeg (ground)
- maple-flavored syrup
- sliced bananas (optional)

### Method:

1. First, beat together eggs, half-and-half, sugar, vanilla, cinnamon and nutmeg in a shallow bowl. Dip bread slices into egg mixture, coating both sides.
2. In a very large skillet or on a griddle, melt 1 tablespoon of the butter over medium heat.
3. Add half of the bread slices and cook for 4 to 6 minutes or until golden, turning once.
4. Repeat with remaining bread slices and the remaining butter.
5. Serve with maple syrup and sliced bananas.

# Vegan Eggnog French Toast with Cracked Cranberry Maple Syrup

Yields: 4-6

## Ingredients:

- 2 tablespoons of canola oil
- 2 cups of vegan eggnog
- 1 tablespoon of pure vanilla extract
- 1 baguette of French bread (sliced into ½ inch thick pieces)
- ¾ cups of soy creamer
- ½ teaspoon of ground cinnamon
- ½ teaspoon of brown sugar
- maple syrup – see the instructions for the amount
- cranberries - see the instructions for the amount
- orange zest - see the instructions for the amount

## Method:

1. First, whisk all of the ingredients (except for the bread, syrup, and cranberries) in a large shallow bowl until well blended.
2. Place as many pieces of bread that will fit into the eggnog mixture and let soak for approximately 1 minute, then flip and soak the other side for 1 minute. *Note:* If the crust is really hard, soak a little longer or until it gives a little when you push on it.
3. Once the bread has soaked on both sides place the pieces on a plate and let them rest for 2 minutes.
4. Lightly coat a large griddle or skillet with 1 tablespoon of the oil and heat on medium high heat.

5. When the pan is hot, place the eggnog-soaked bread slices flat side down in the pan and cook until they are golden brown, approximately two minutes. Flip and cook the other side until golden brown.

6. If you're cooking for a large group transfer to a warm oven until ready to serve.

*Maple Syrup with Cracked Cranberries:*

1. Warm the syrup (approximately ¼ cup per serving) in a pan on low heat. Add 6 cranberries per ¼ cup and heat them until they crack open. Serve warm over the French toast.

2. Grate orange zest over the top of the French toast and syrup.

# W

## Waffle French Toast

Yield: 4 waffles

**Ingredient
s:**

- 16 (1/2-inch-thick) slices day-old French bread (about 7 ounces)
- 2 medium-large eggs
- 1 tablespoon butter (melted)
- 1 teaspoon vanilla extract
- 1 cup fat-free milk
- 1 tablespoon sugar
- ½ teaspoon ground cinnamon
- cooking spray

**Method:**

1. Coat waffle iron with cooking spray, and preheat.
2. Combine milk, eggs, butter, vanilla extract, sugar, and cinnamon, stirring well with a whisk.
3. Place bread in a 13 x 9-inch baking dish; pour milk mixture over bread, turning to coat. Let stand 5 minutes.
4. Place 4 bread slices on hot waffle iron. Cook 3 to 5 minutes or until done; repeat the procedure with the remaining bread.

# Wentelteefjes (Dutch French Toast)

Serves: 2-4

## Ingredients:

- 8 slices day-old white bread
- 2 medium-large eggs (lightly beaten)
- 2 tablespoons icing sugar
- 1 ½ ounces butter (more if needed)
- 1 ½ cups lukewarm milk
- 1 teaspoon cinnamon
- ½ teaspoon vanilla extract
- ¼-½ teaspoon lemon zest (grated)
- extra icing sugar, to serve (confectioner's sugar)
- salt, to season

## Method:

1. First, whisk the milk in a bowl with the lightly beaten eggs, a pinch of salt, the icing sugar, lemon zest, and vanilla extract.
2. Remove the crusts from the bread, and lay the slices in a shallow dish.
3. Pour the milk mixture over the bread and let stand for 30 minutes.
4. Melt the butter in a skillet and fry the bread slices on both sides until golden, being careful they don't break.
5. Serve immediately, sprinkled with extra icing sugar and cinnamon.

# Conclusion

Once again, I genuinely want to thank you for purchasing this book.

As we know, traditional French toast was first made by simply dipping slices of bread in egg or milk, and then fried in butter – creating a simple, yet delicious, desert.

But over the years, this humble dish has seen several gourmet makeovers. Chefs from across the globe have experimented with a variety of ingredients, creating some of the most decadent and delicious French toast recipes known to man.

Even more recently, French toast has evolved into a savory sandwich, known as the Monte Cristo.

An evolution of the croque-monsieur, this delicious and crustless sandwich is full to the brim with ham and cheese, buttered and then lightly browned on both sides in a skillet or under a broiler – this truly is a must have for any French toast enthusiast.

And the list of recipes goes on.

From savoury to sweet, from breakfast to desert, French toast is the perfect food for every occasion – and as a bonus, it is also extremely easy to make!

There is a very good reason that French toast has genuinely stood the test of time, acting as a dietary staple for centuries and with an extensive history in French culture.

And now they are all in the palm of your hand, just waiting to be explored.

So again, what are you waiting for?

Thank you, and please enjoy!

# Other Books by Grizzly Publishing

*"Jamaican Cookbook: Traditional Jamaican Recipes Made Easy"*

https://www.amazon.com/dp/B07B68KL8D

*"Brazilian Instant Pot Cookbook: Delicious Pressure Cooked Meals Made Fast and Easy"*
https://www.amazon.com/dp/B078XBYP89

*"Norwegian Cookbook: Traditional Scandinavian Recipes Made Easy"*

https://www.amazon.com/dp/B079M2W223

*"Casserole Cookbook: Delicious Casserole Recipes From Around The World"*

https://www.amazon.com/dp/B07B6GV61Q

.